25 Days of Christmas

Printed by Createspace

ISBN: 978-1540574046

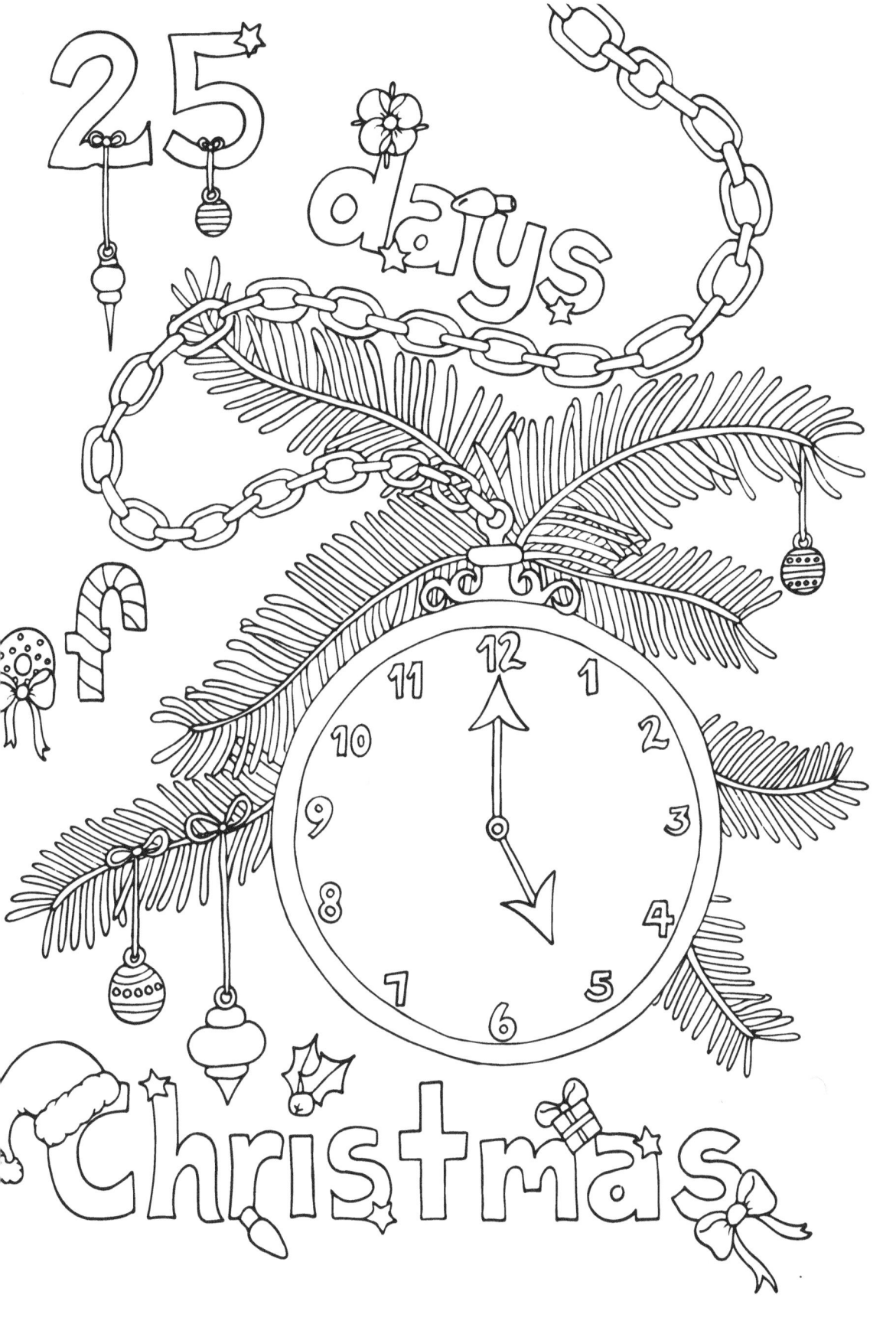

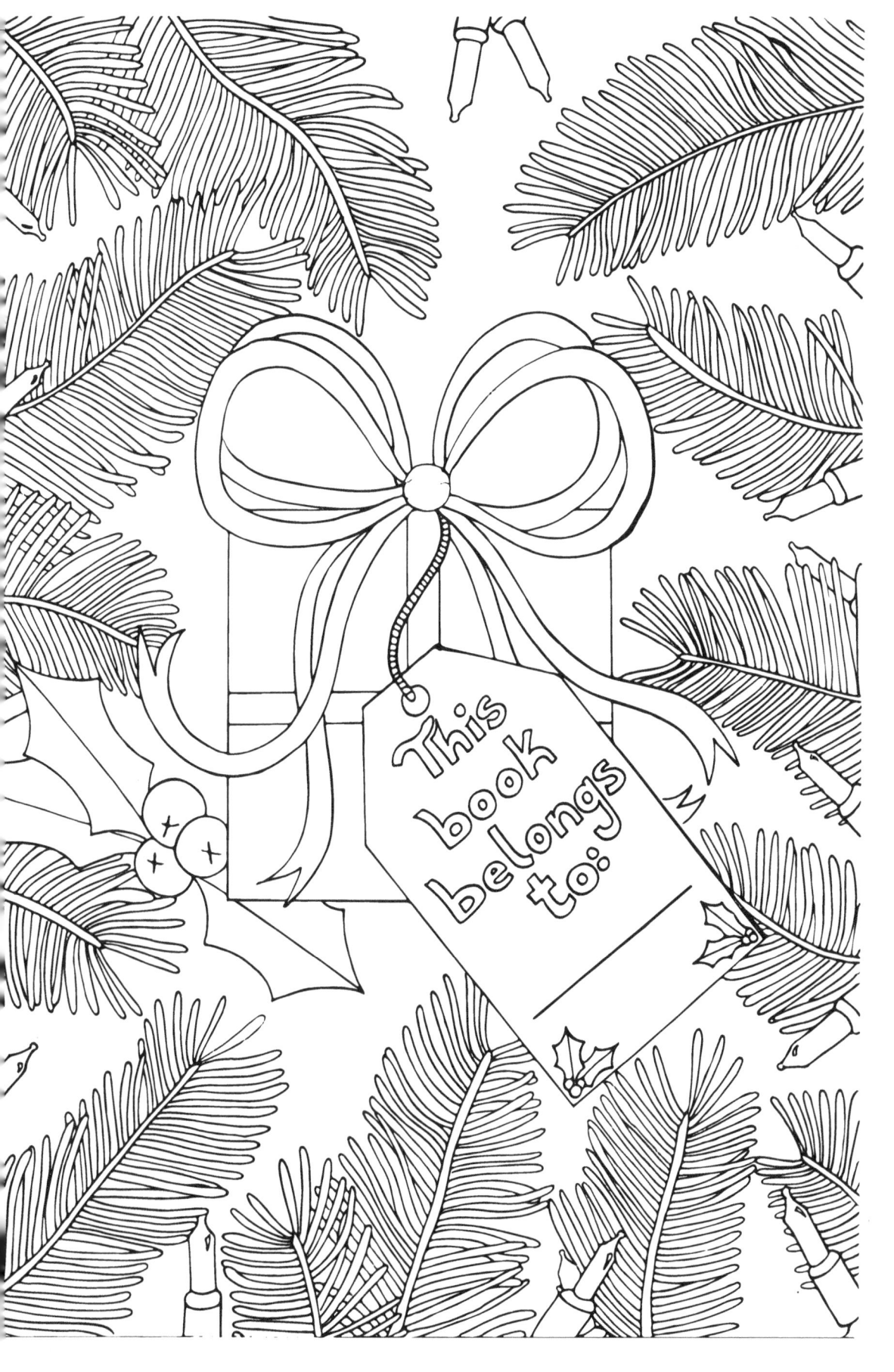

This book belongs to:

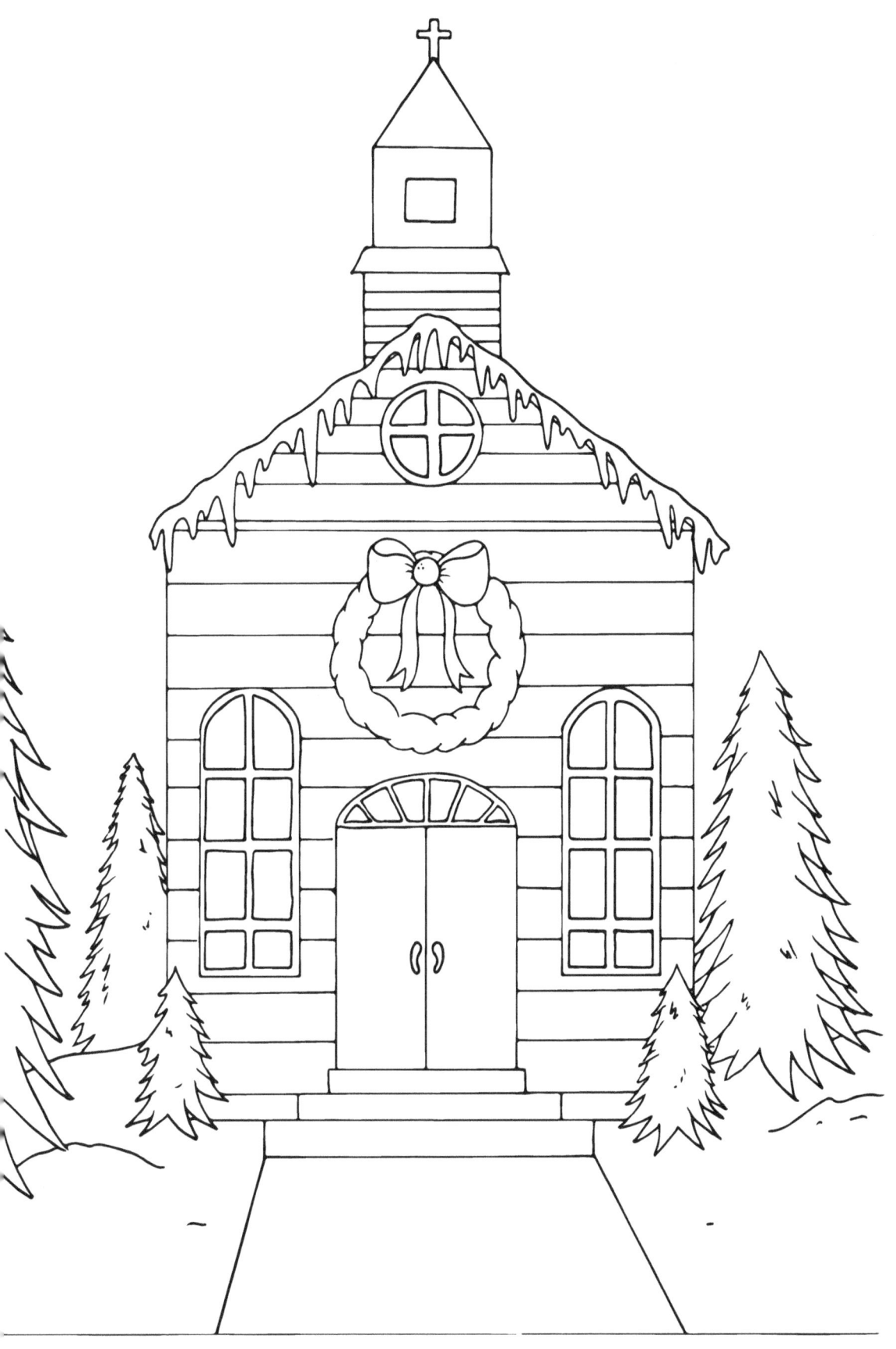

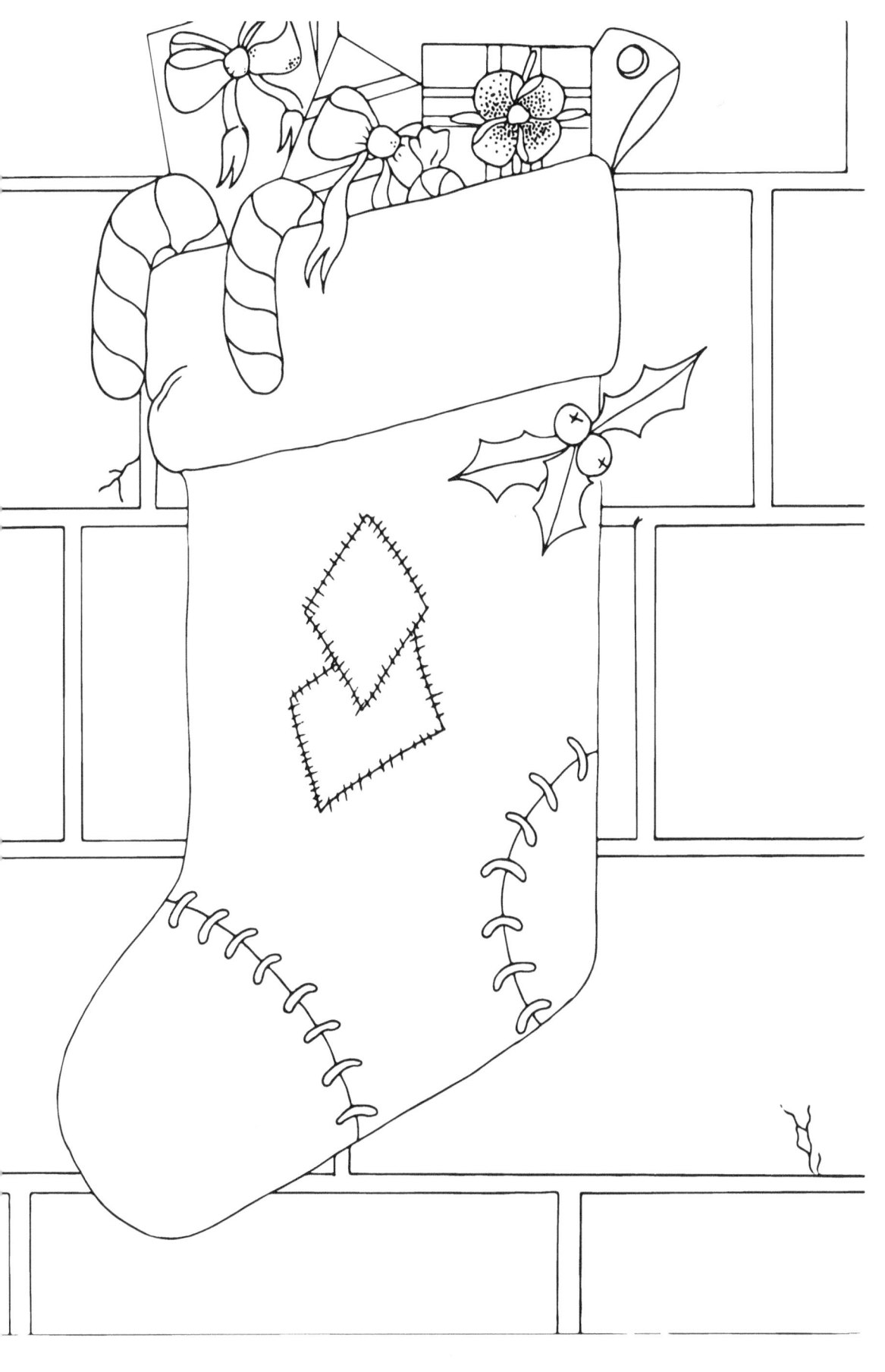

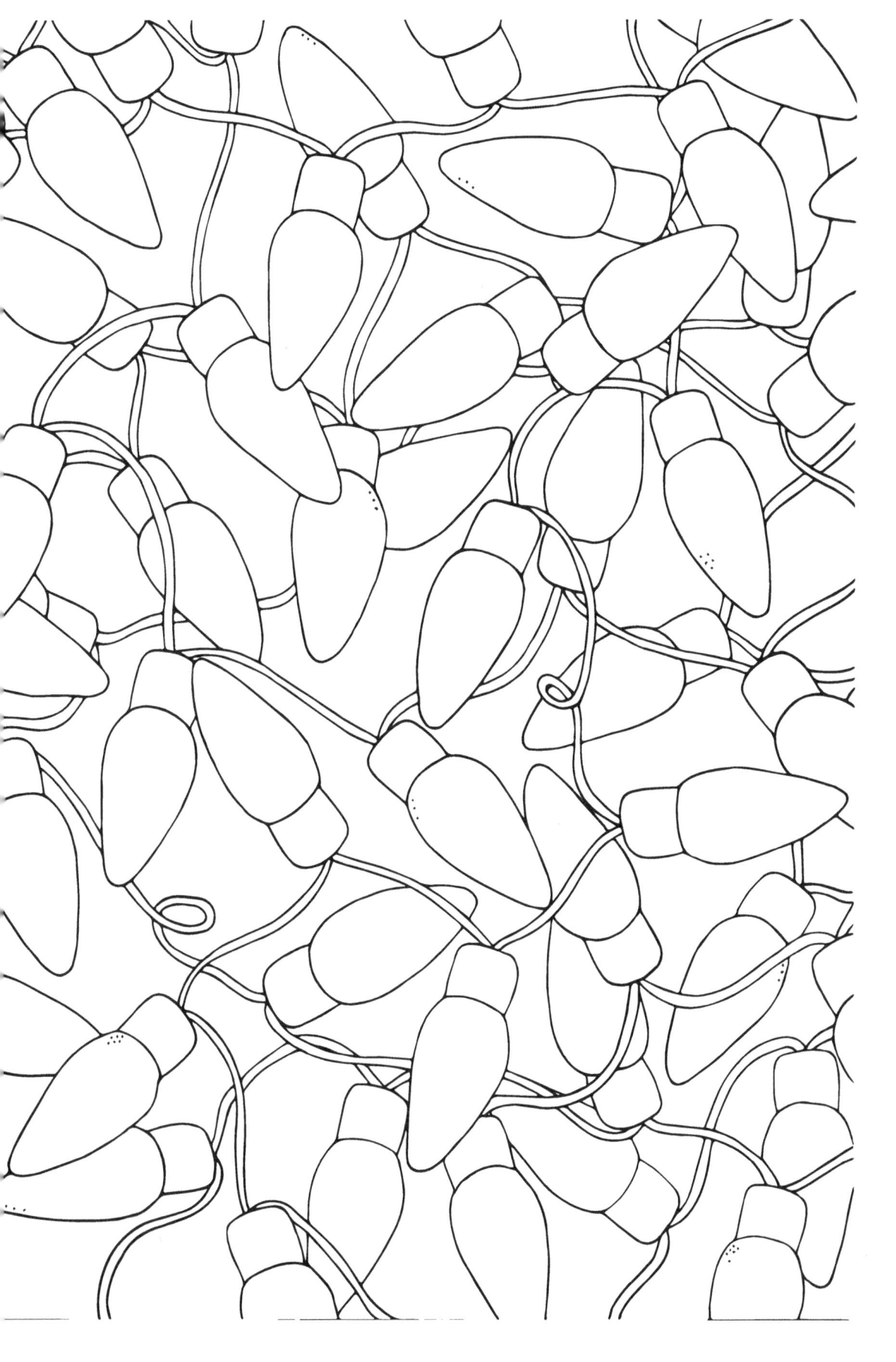

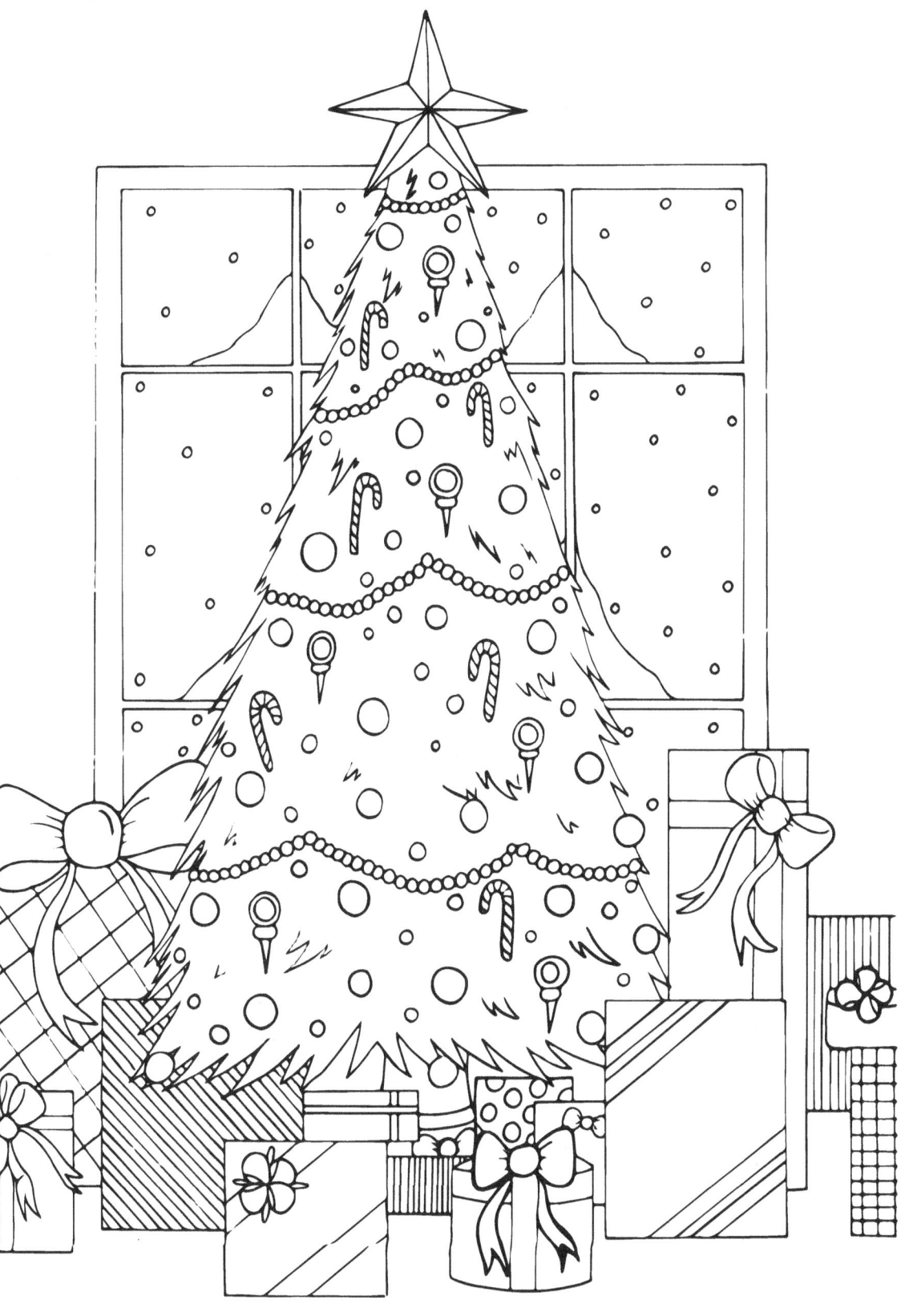

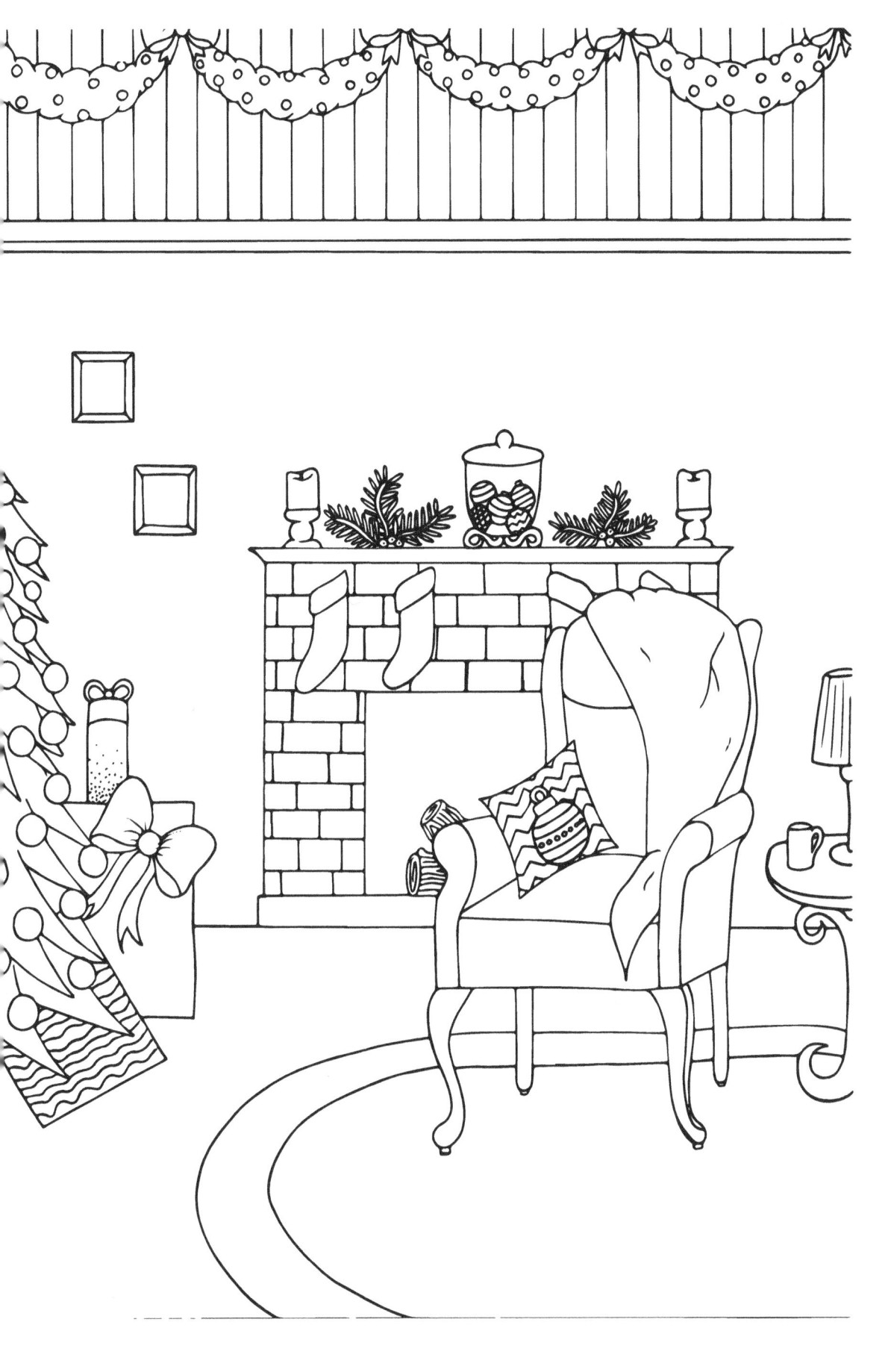

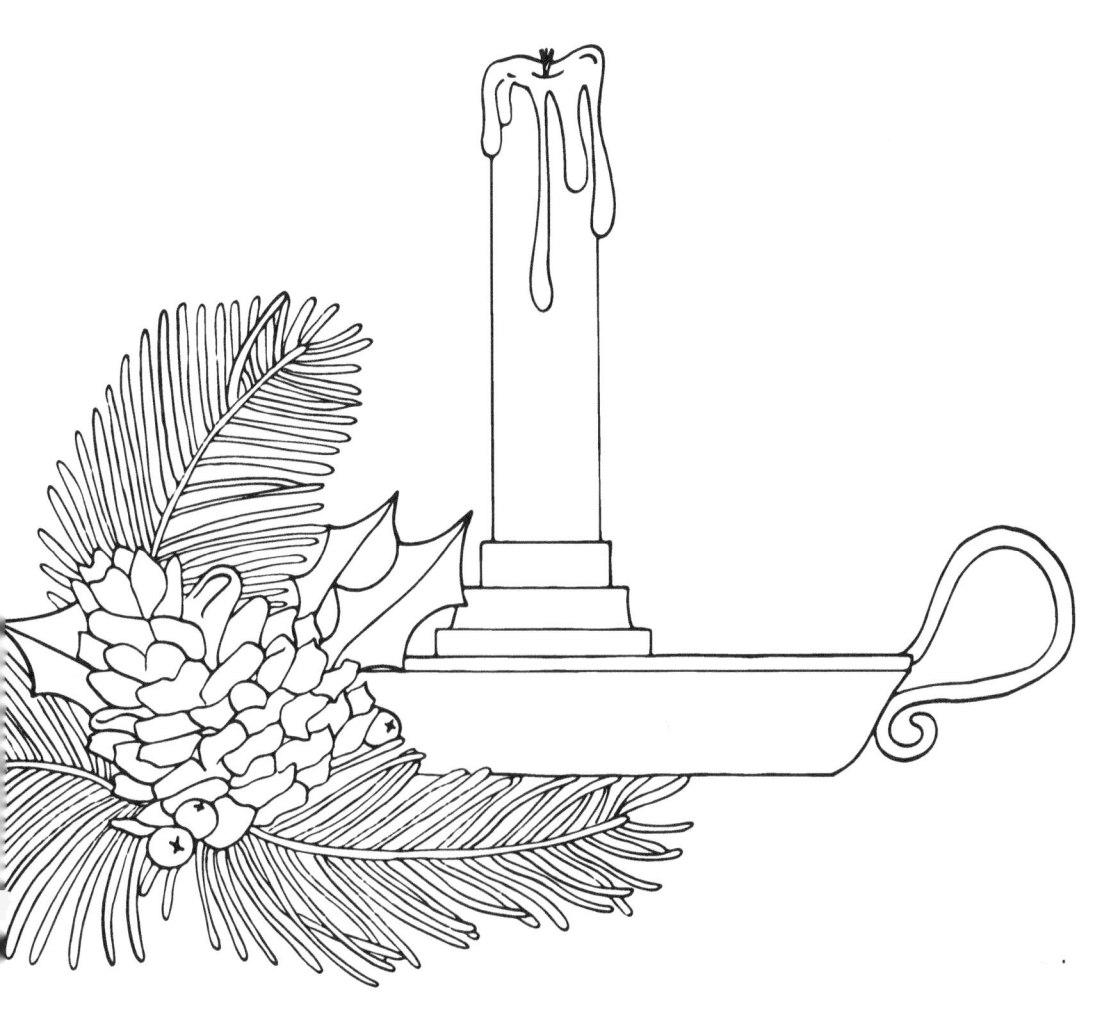

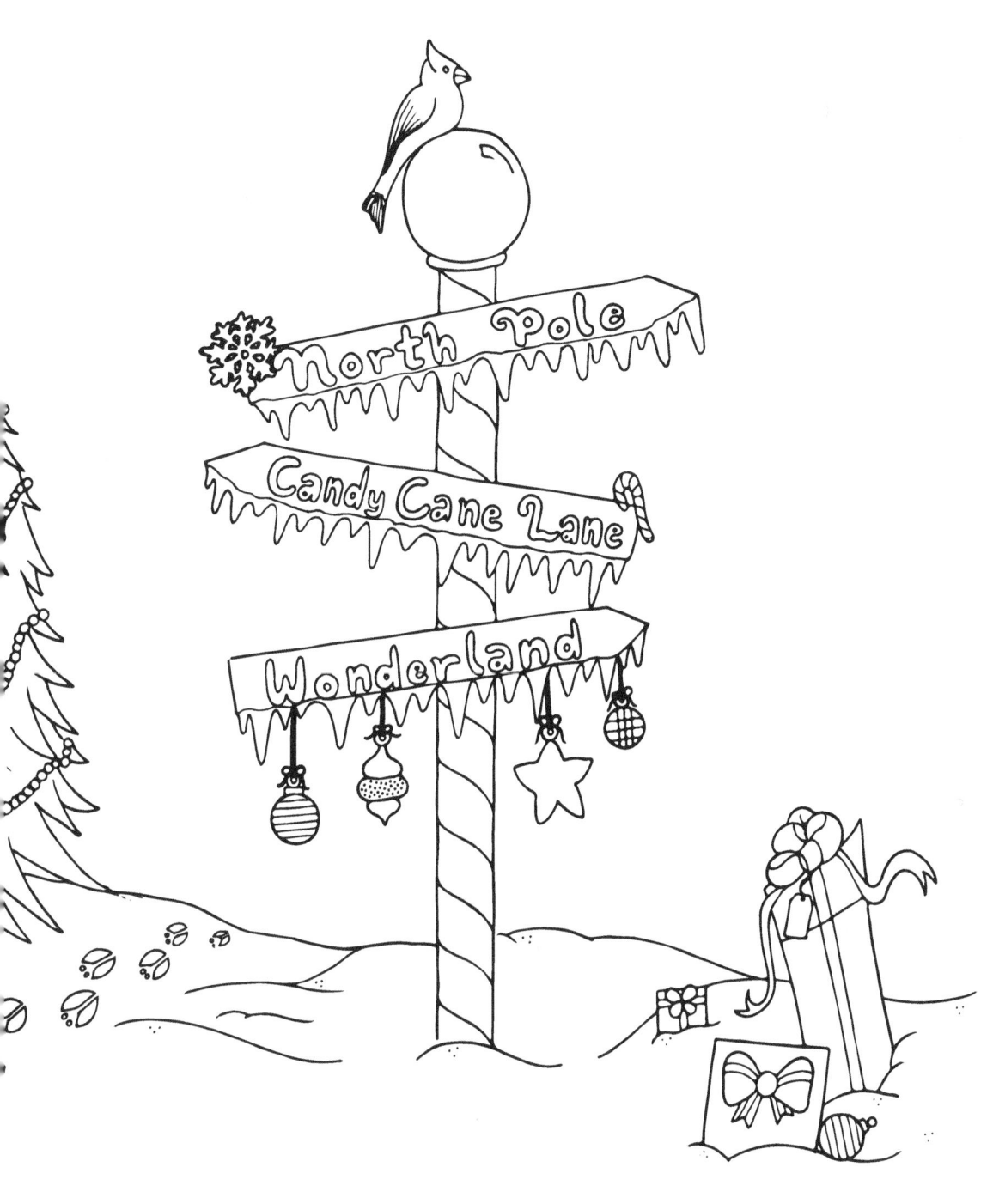

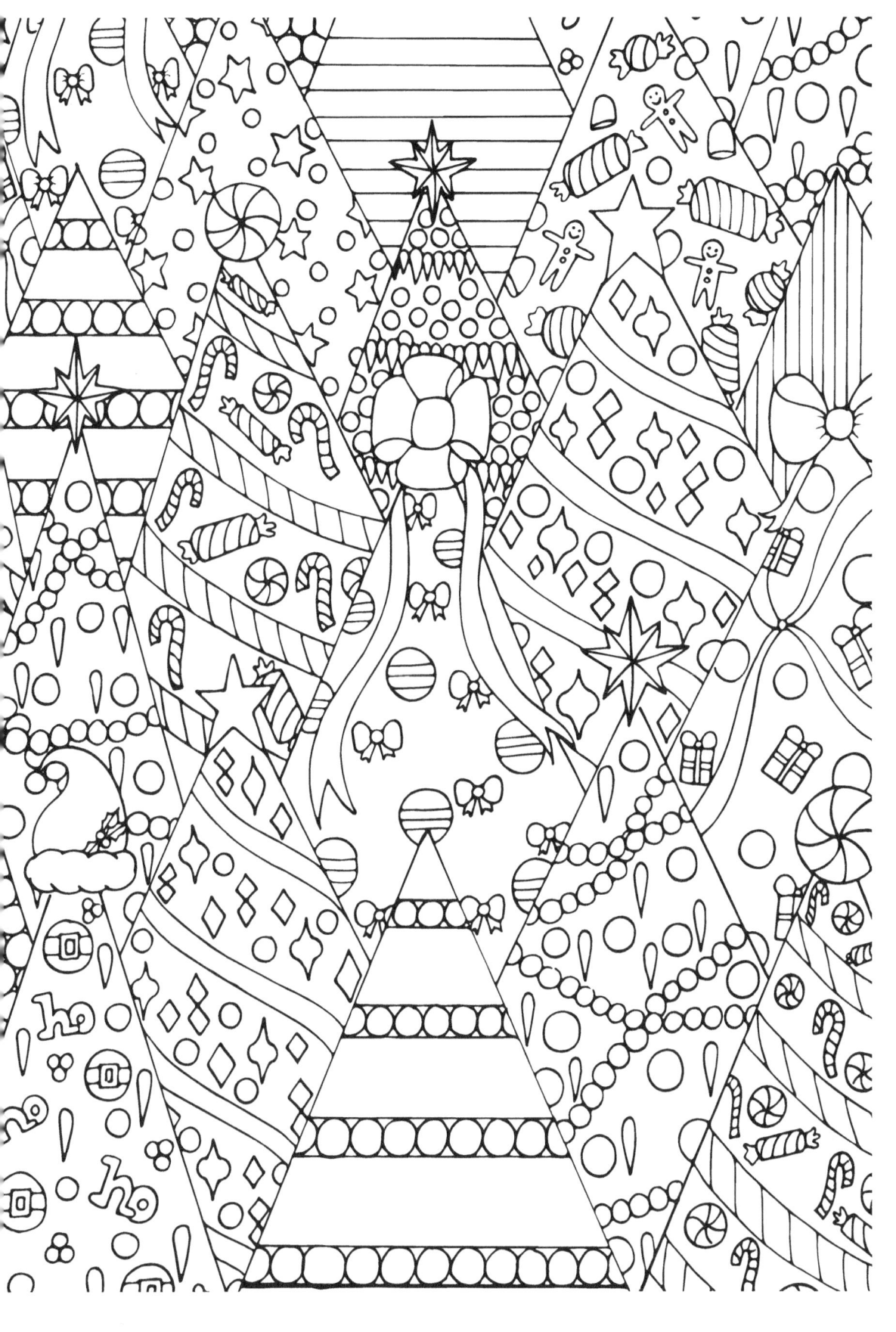

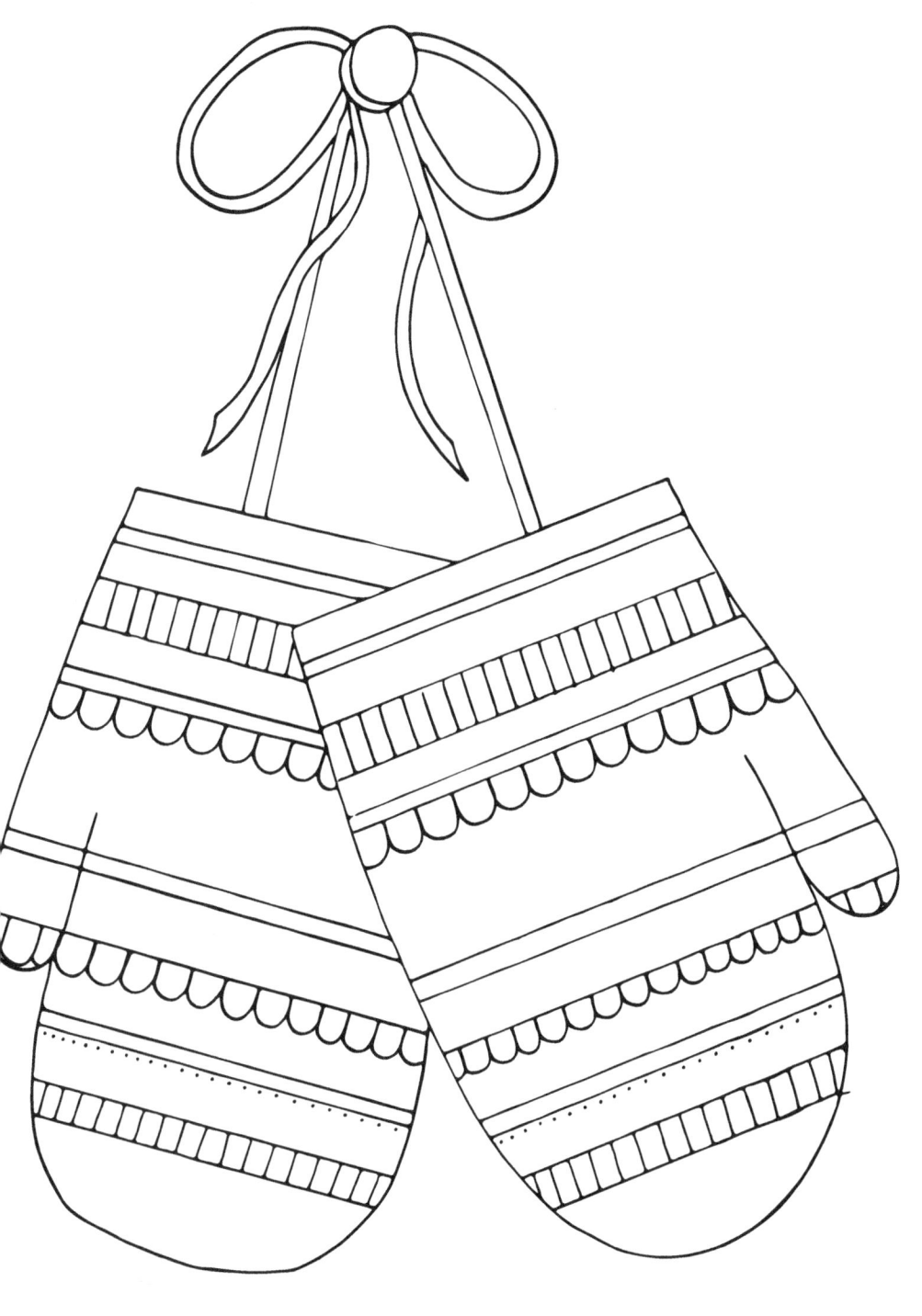

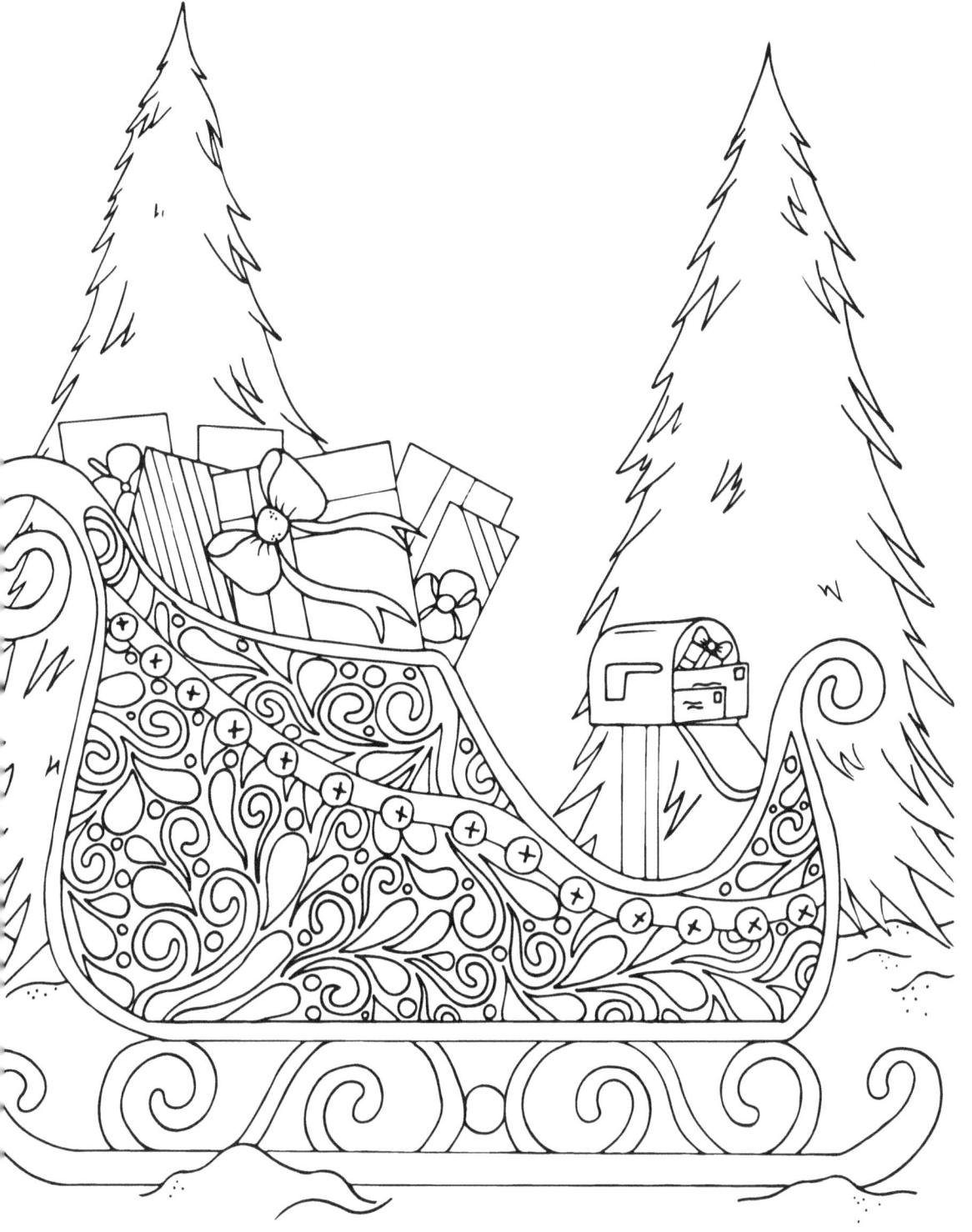

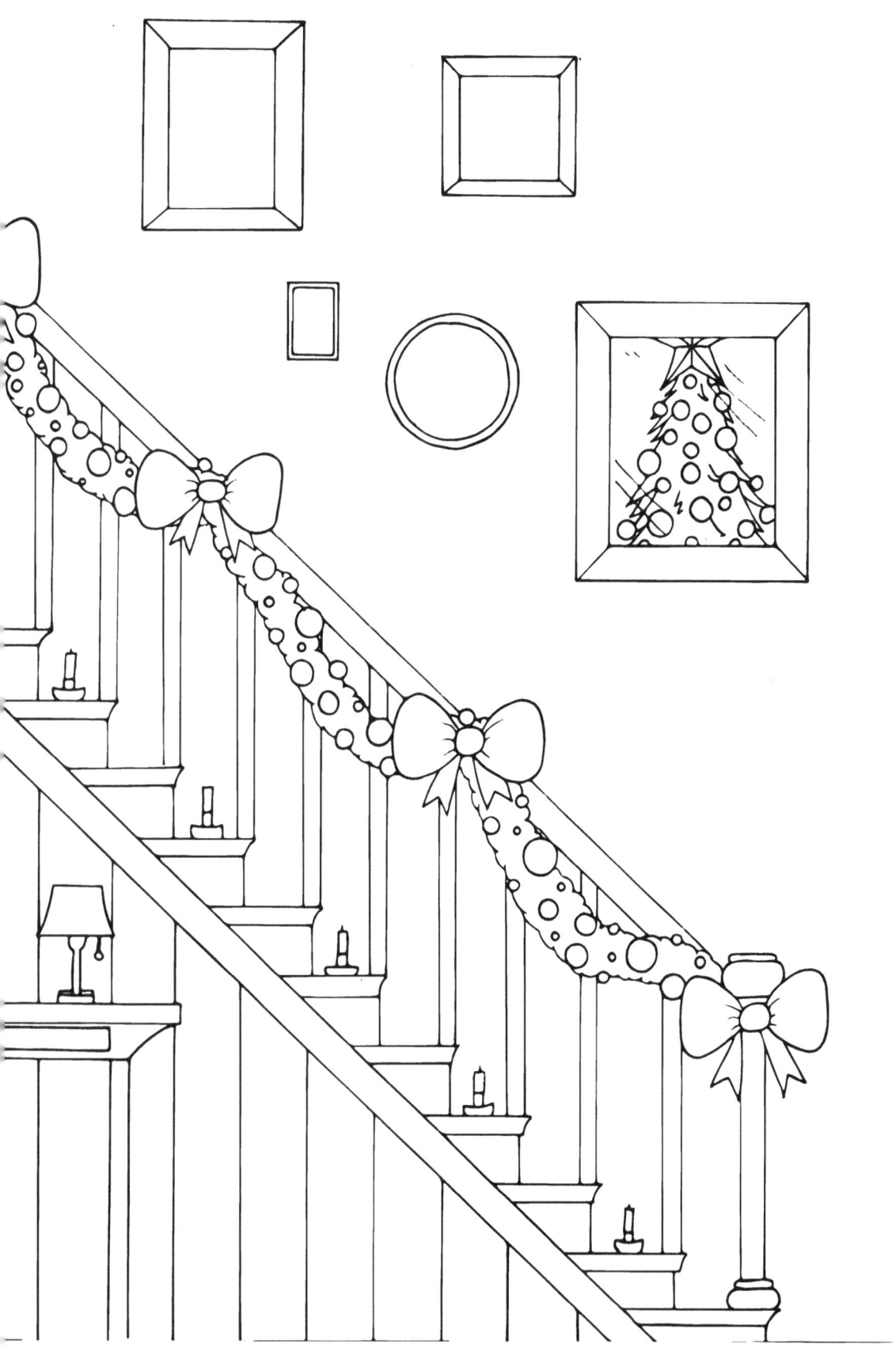

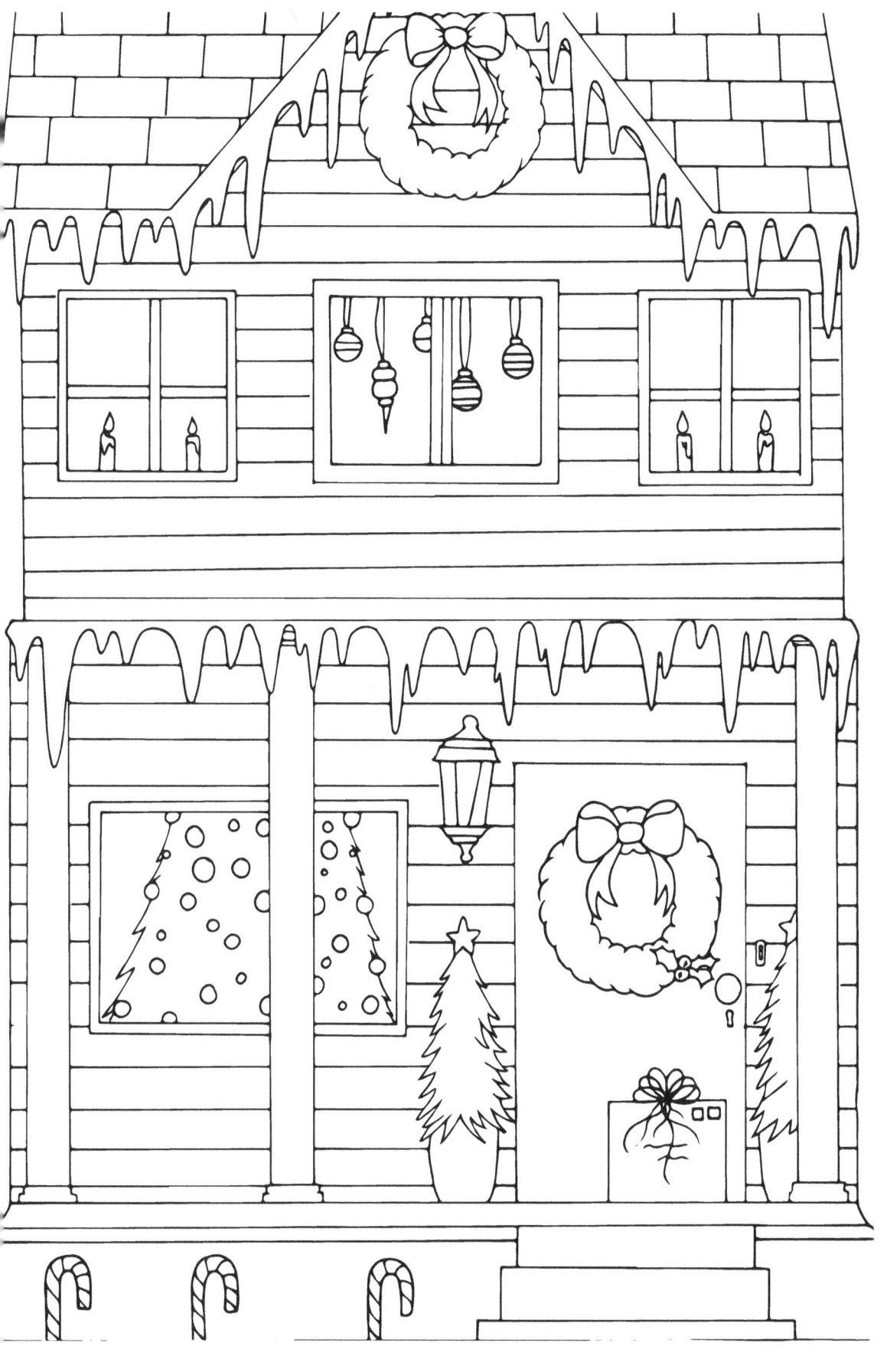

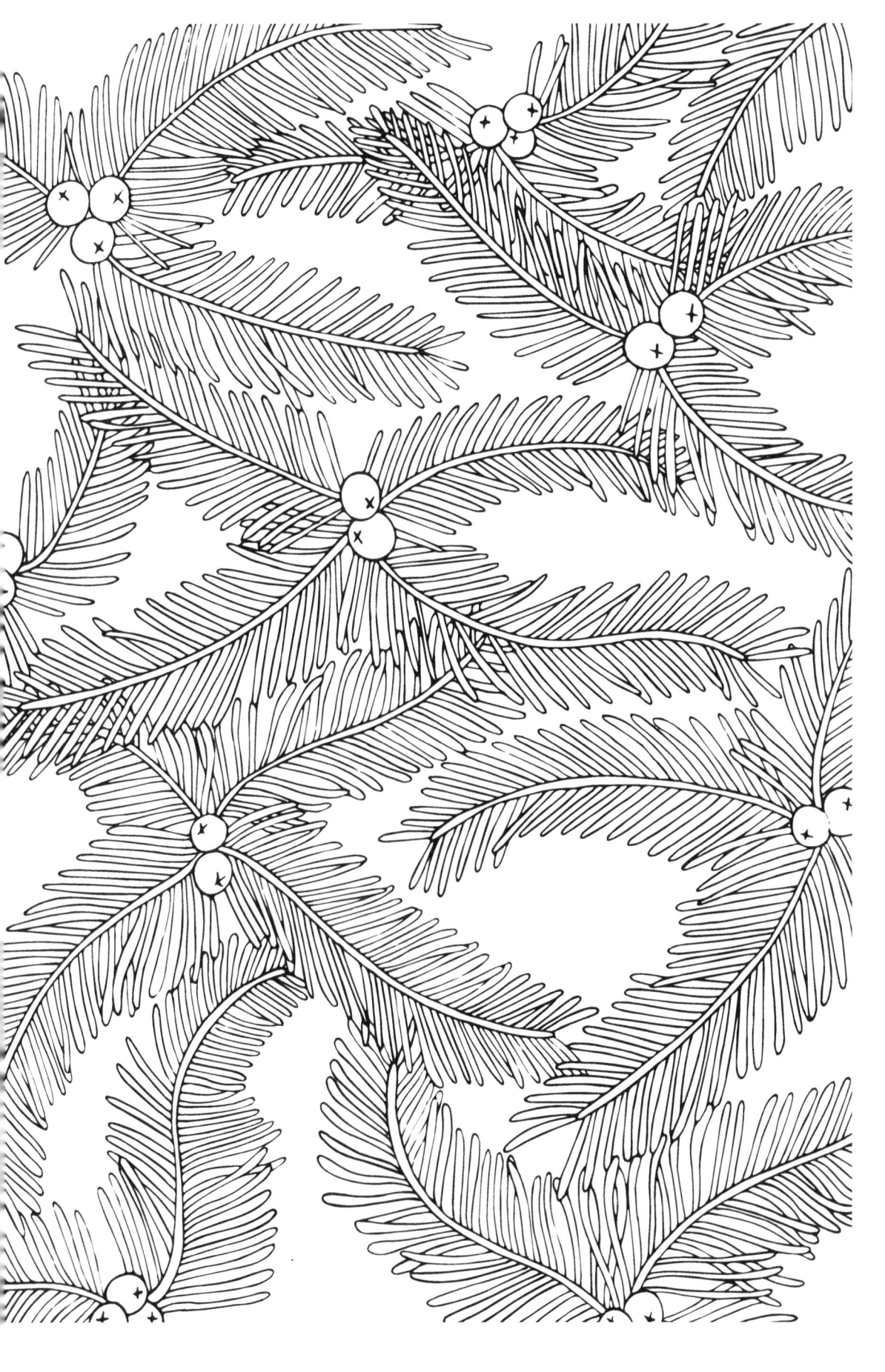

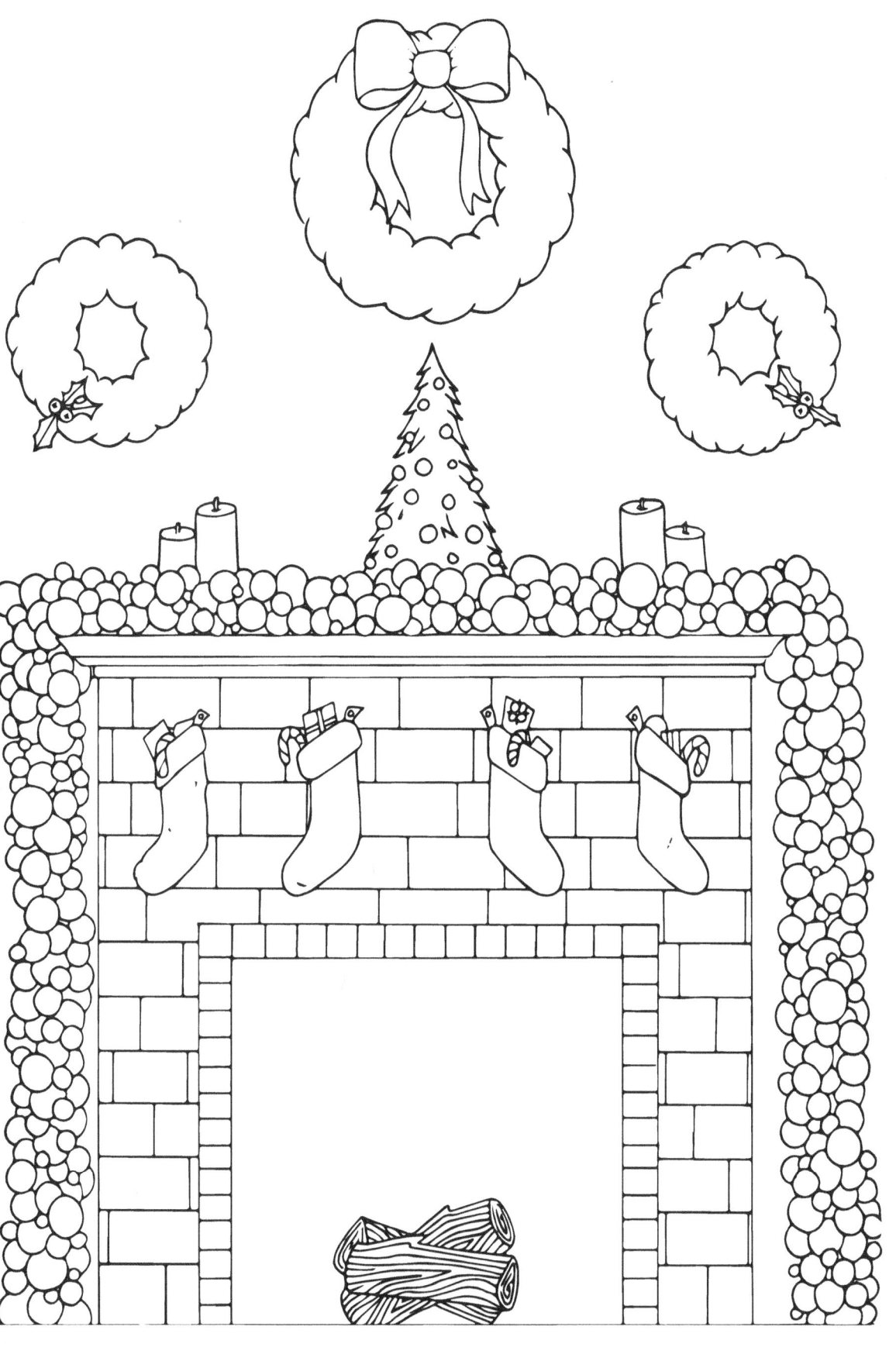

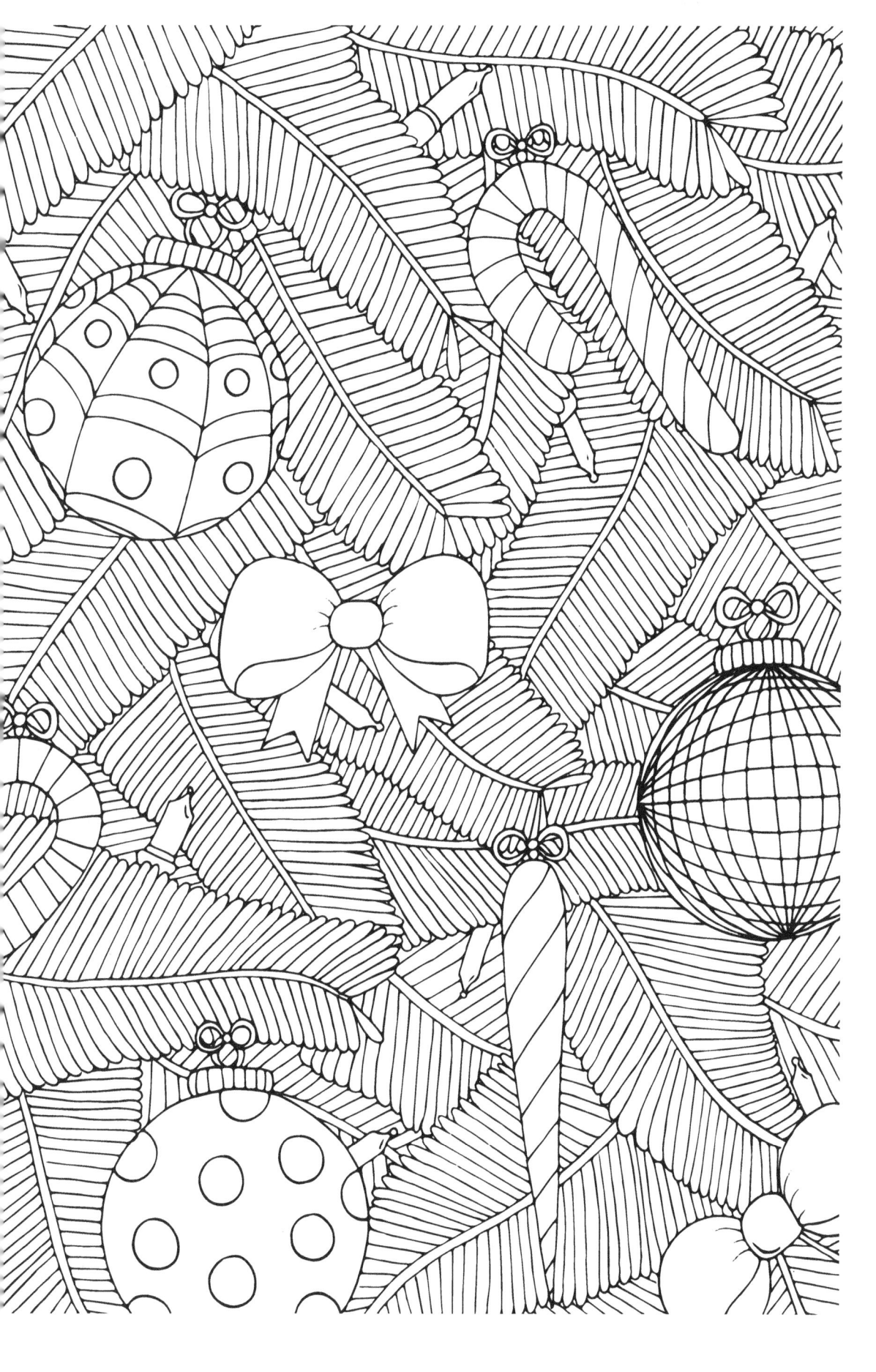

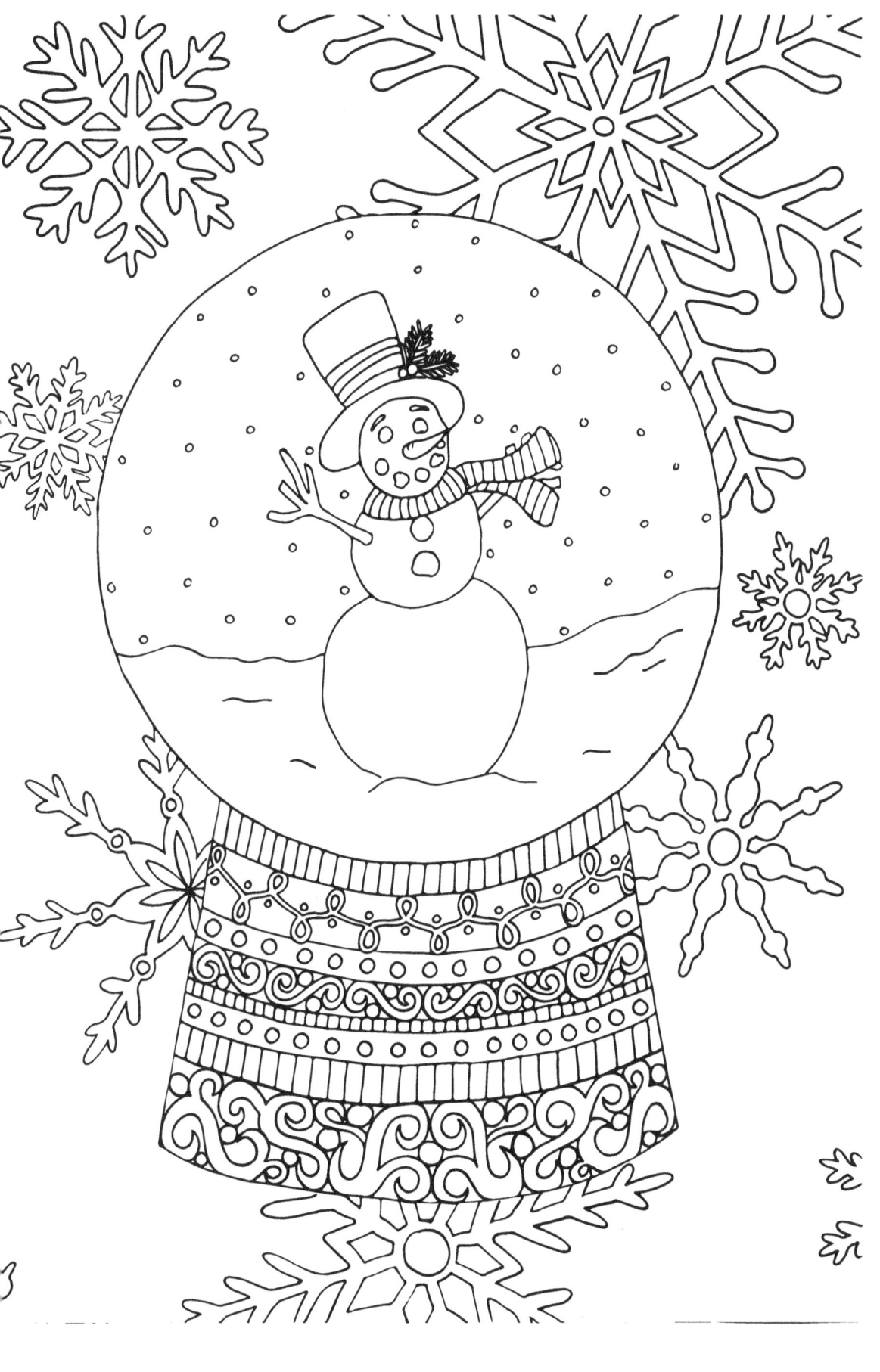

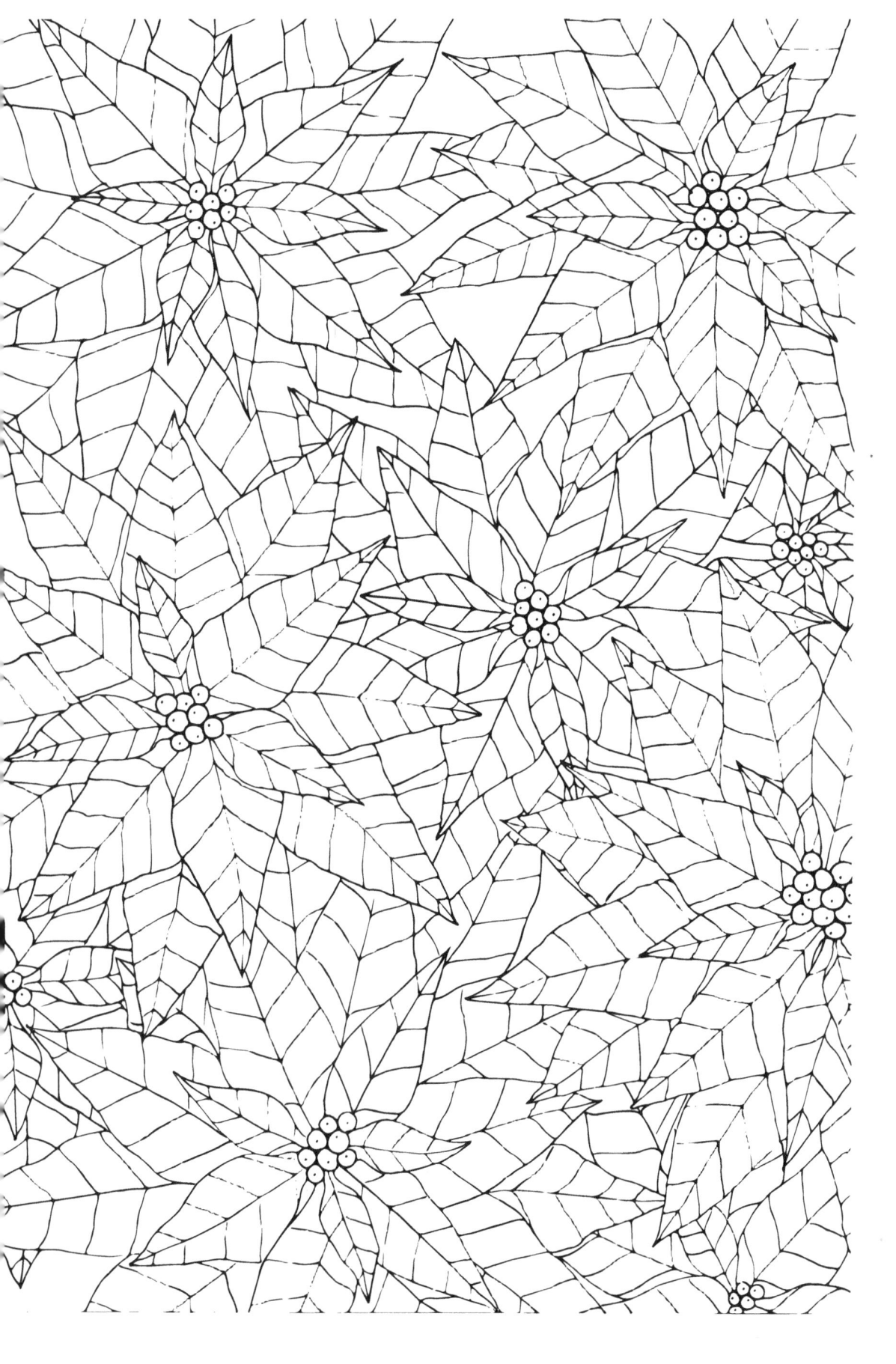

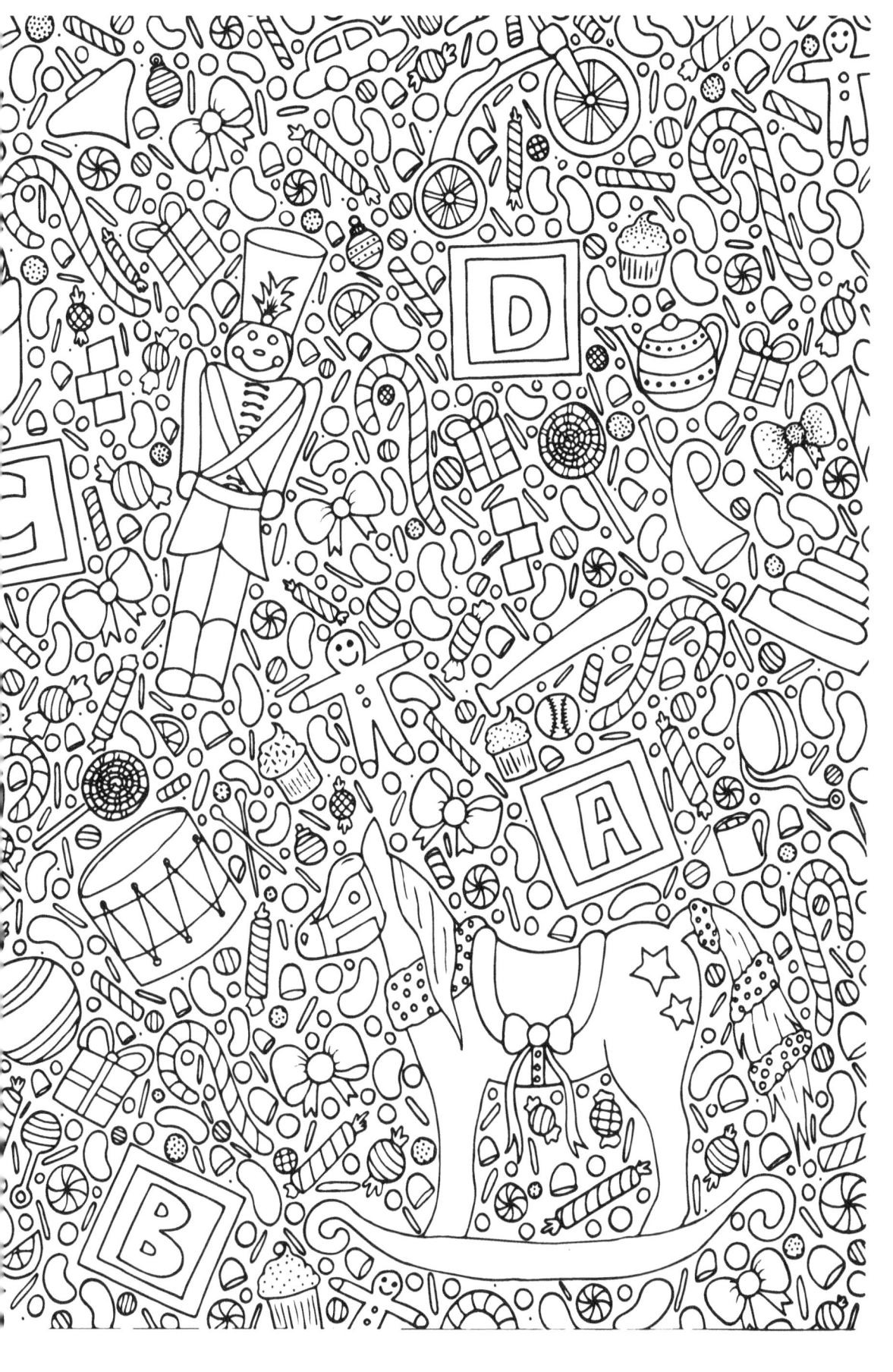

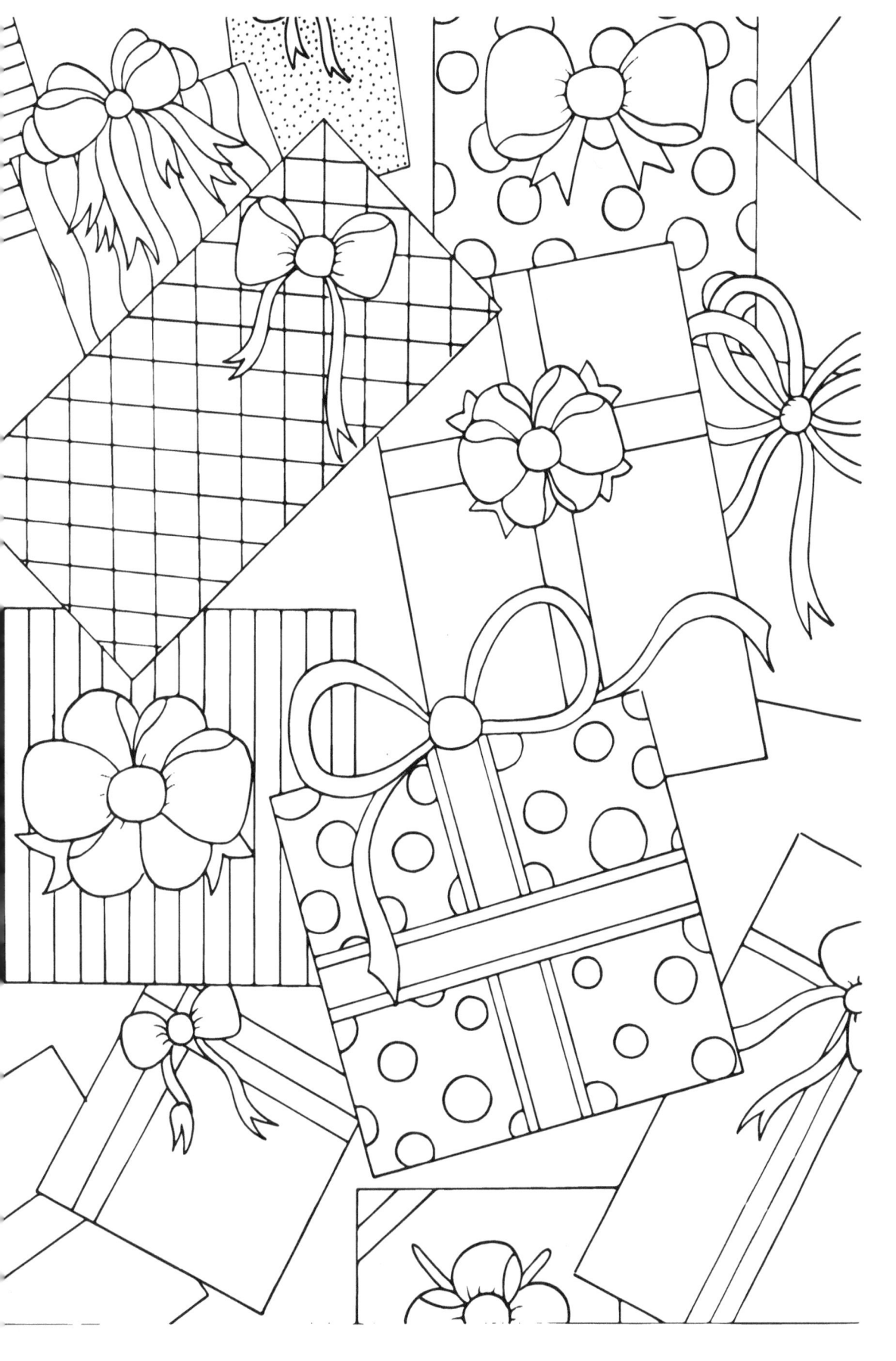

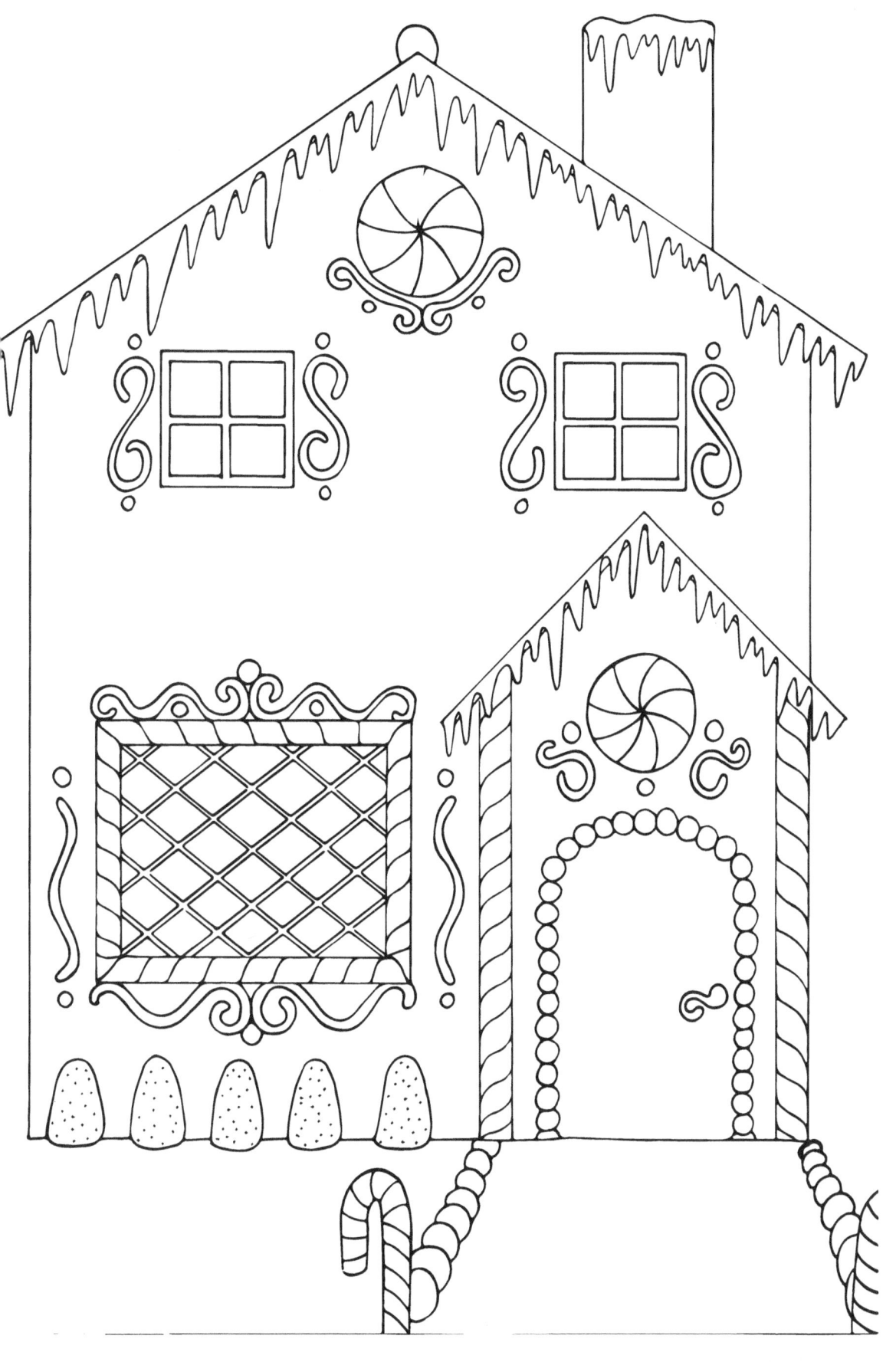

www.ingramcontent.com/pod-product-compliance
Lightning Source LLC
Chambersburg PA
CBHW081754280526
45789CB00008B/2851